HER

Her

JOE RINEHART

jwrino1@gmail.com

ISBN 9798218107598

Edited and designed by Tell Tell Poetry

Printed in the United States of America

First Printing, December 2022

TABLE OF CONTENTS

ACKNOWLEDGMENTS

"Soft Spot" - Published in Qua Literary and Fine Arts Magazine, Fall 2021

Ladies and Gentlemen,

The story of Her...

Her

HERE FOREVER, TODAY

I've been
Stumbling around
Until I found you
You have a big smile,
on the front of you
A swagger unknown to mankind

I ask where you're from, babe
You must be straight from the Heavens
Girl, I won't go anywhere
Because I'm here forever, today

This love is so divine
I'm so glad you're mine
I could
Lay on this couch all day
But, enjoy it for now

Where are you going, babe?
You must be
Straight from the Heavens
Girl, I won't go anywhere
Because I'm here forever, today

RING

I wasn't
Doing any forever shopping
I don't
Think I've ever thought about this before!

I want to
Buy you something one day
That
Tells you that you're mine forever, hey!

I need you
To never ever leave my house
On the mind all the time
I'll be here forever, forget the day!

I want to
Buy you something one day
That
Tells you that you're mine forever, hey!

PANDEMIC

Something isn't right...

Pandemic

At home academic, scholar

This feeling is becoming an epidemic,
holler, at you,

Hollering is louder, I can feel this feeling even more
it's like every two,

Two hours I am checking my phone it's been
a while since I've heard from her

It spreads even quicker like COVID,
drifting back to feelings of when I was nineteen

Maybe I'll be over this, over my head,
drifting back when I get away from her.
The movie is restarting, there's the screen

PANDEMIC PT. 2

These FaceTimes are getting annoying

I don't think you care anymore,

that's soul-destroying

My love is truly authentic

Somehow we both stay invested in our academics

I feel like you'd prefer that

instead of dealing with me, I'm like a rat

I'm a nuisance, I can tell

I'm scared to ask and hear what you'll tell

BLISS & TUMBLING

I am clueless
Miles away
Blinded by bliss
So happy even in a pandemic
I wish I could run to you, even shoeless
All that just to say hey
I just need a quick kiss
I am blinded by bliss running like I'm schizophrenic

...

I hate Kroger
And I hate T-Mobile
I thought "damn I really lost her"
Tumbling and I'm falling faster
In love, but won't tell me
This has to be temporary
Haven't slept in weeks
Not a good technique
I like not eating
For twenty four hours
I keep on repeating
I've lost will power

PARTY

All of your friends wanted a hug
I feel like I have a stomach bug
Way too much to drink, as I trip over the rug
Even had a few puffs of the green drug

Another thing,
Some friend you have there
I don't get passed around like cards in solitaire
I was fresh and new to the market to be fair

All of a sudden,
I'm blacked out
Can't be pumped up by Joe Budden
Half eaten taco falling from my mouth

Do we need therapy?
I mean, our road has become bumpy
I'm just so upset and grumpy, in this moment
Forgive me and my dramatic moments

BROKEN PHONE GLASS

I threw that son of a bitch across the room
Right off my dresser, it made a loud boom
In the air it made an audible zoom
Went from a light room to a dark room

Tears well up
If I had make-up,
it would be messed up
New phone bill just went up

To the floor, I go down
This is the way it went down?
Pick up my phone, it's okay, set it down
Those tears on my face moved down

Call someone...
only if your phone works

FRONT YARD

Oh, baby it wasn't too hard
Look at me now I'm in my front yard
All in and no self regard
Look at me I'm in my front yard

I know you have a few spies, sneaky like a cat
I thought I'd let them have that
I can tell you she's really something to look at
I hit a home run with this, used a baseball bat

Oh, baby it wasn't too hard
Look at me now I'm in my front yard
All in and no self regard
Look at me I'm in my front yard

I like to party with her,
that's all you need to know
Movies, shows, puffs, she has an afterglow
Didn't go far for a rebound, not to Chicago
But she turned cold like the Pack in Lambeau

WITH OR WITHOUT YOU

I am doing fine on my own
Really it's no big deal
You shouldn't have to worry about me
I mean,
Going to school, working, and getting my degree
I knew I could do this with or without you
I can do it with someone else too, even temporarily
...
Miller lite
I still hate this night
3am, no daylight
I'm not the rebound type
Blocked on everything; out of sight
This was too easy the way I made it right
I flew myself up to the door like a kite
I told her, "You aren't really my type."
She said, "I'll change that, I just might."
Please, stop trying to make me
put my arm around you
I've realized my mistake tonight
Should've left it at the door

WHERE TO NOW?

Park the silver bullet in the driveway

It's 9 o'clock on a Sunday

By the way, happy birthday

I figured I'd swing by your way

I delivered your care package

To celebrate your new age

I don't get to help with your special dinner

The graphic shirts I bought shimmer

under your porch lights

Now I drive around

aimlessly

I listen to my radio sound, shamefully

I ask, where to now?

CARED TOO MUCH

I cared too much for us
You caught the nearest bus
To get the hell out
Now all I do is pout
I want our feeling back
I want your weight off my back

It's only been a couple months man
Just a couple months and you stay rent free
Just a couple months since we tried to get a tan
Just a couple months since I heard you say
you loved me

All that time talking waiting for me to
say something
Say something back to retaliate
Fuck the rhyme scheme, this is real

No arguments, no problems
No arguments, no excitement
"Speak up," she said

I cared for us too much

TUMBLING & BLISS

So badly I want to die
My room is a pigsty
Please just answer my calls
What a mistake after all

Knock on my door and enter hell
I told you I'm not even well
Unless you want me to be well
Don't let me blow up like a fuel cell

Drinking my beer
No one wants to hear me talk
I'll be telling everyone the same thing
to hear
So to the streets I will jaywalk

I sit on my floor
Close myself off, no open door
Liquor goes easier than before
And my room ceilings are drawing in smoke like a war

WORLDWIDE

I've been getting around I guess you could say
Nothing I'd consider the wrong way
You could say that I'm worldwide

No one quite does the trick for me anymore
You're stuck upstairs on the second floor
I could really use a knife to cut out this feeling,
open the drawer

I've been getting around I guess you could say
Nothing I'd consider the wrong way
You could say that I'm worldwide

Life sucks and I could've used a do-over with her
Feelings of it make shiver like it's December
Except I don't get the gift of a good
relationship tenure, outside of you

I've been getting around I guess you could say
Nothing I'd consider the wrong way
You could say that I'm worldwide

THE CONVERSATION

Clear as day
Put the bottle away
Put the substance away
Put the feelings away
I can see all now

The world doesn't revolve around her
Even though you wanted forever with her
Even though you wanted to tell her you loved her
Can't let that slip around her

Clear as day
Put the bottle away
Put the substance away
Put the feelings away
I can see all now

Life is a little bit better when you are alive
Just make sure you do it cautiously
Like when you go on your walks,
Watch out for the potholes
Those can set you back

CLOTHES

I can't wear that hat comfortably
Not with this future I've moved into
But certainly,
I'll keep it, no matter how much I may feel blue

I can't wear this shirt comfortably
Not with the way the past is
But definitely,
I'll keep it, no matter how annoying it is

SOFT SPOT

I saw you on Dixie the other day
I thought about honking at you and just saying hey
But I was on the clock busy getting my pay
I also saw your second man since me
Did some investigating, he looks just like me
Mop top, skinny boned, really large tee
Makes me remember you still have one of my shirts
If I'm not mistaken I think that it's a sweatshirt
I bet you sleep in it, I bet it's your nightshirt
I still have some bobby pins and some other shit
Mac shirts and tan hats, you bought all of it
You did love me and you meant all of...*cool it man*

FOREVER

There were nights where I never slept
There were days where I never ate and just wept
Your magic trick was hard to accept
Disappearing acts create some disrespect
Somewhere though, I'll still love you forever

I hear that you're happy without me
You've completed finally
a lifelong fantasy
I hope you both think it's meant to be
Somewhere though, I'll still love you forever

I'd die for you still, I think
I hope you found that missing link
I had to doublethink the first line
If you showed up crying, I'd let you in
Because somewhere, I'll still love you forever

ABOUT THE WRITER

Joe Rinehart was born in Waterford, Michigan in the year 2000. While piling up several poems after finding a love for poetry, Rinehart realized he wanted to share it with the world. After publishing “Soft Spot” in the Qua Literary and Fine Arts Magazine in the Fall of 2021, he realized how powerful poetry can be. When he isn’t working, studying, or writing, Rinehart commonly travels to Manistee, Michigan, and continuously writes to perfect his craft. Rinehart’s poetry often questions the mechanisms of the world and abstract emotions making any reader feel comfortable while enjoying his poetry.

www.ingramcontent.com/pod-product-compliance
Lightning Source LLC
LaVergne TN
LVHW020535160826
845677LV00015B/4066

* 9 7 9 8 2 1 8 1 0 7 5 9 8 *